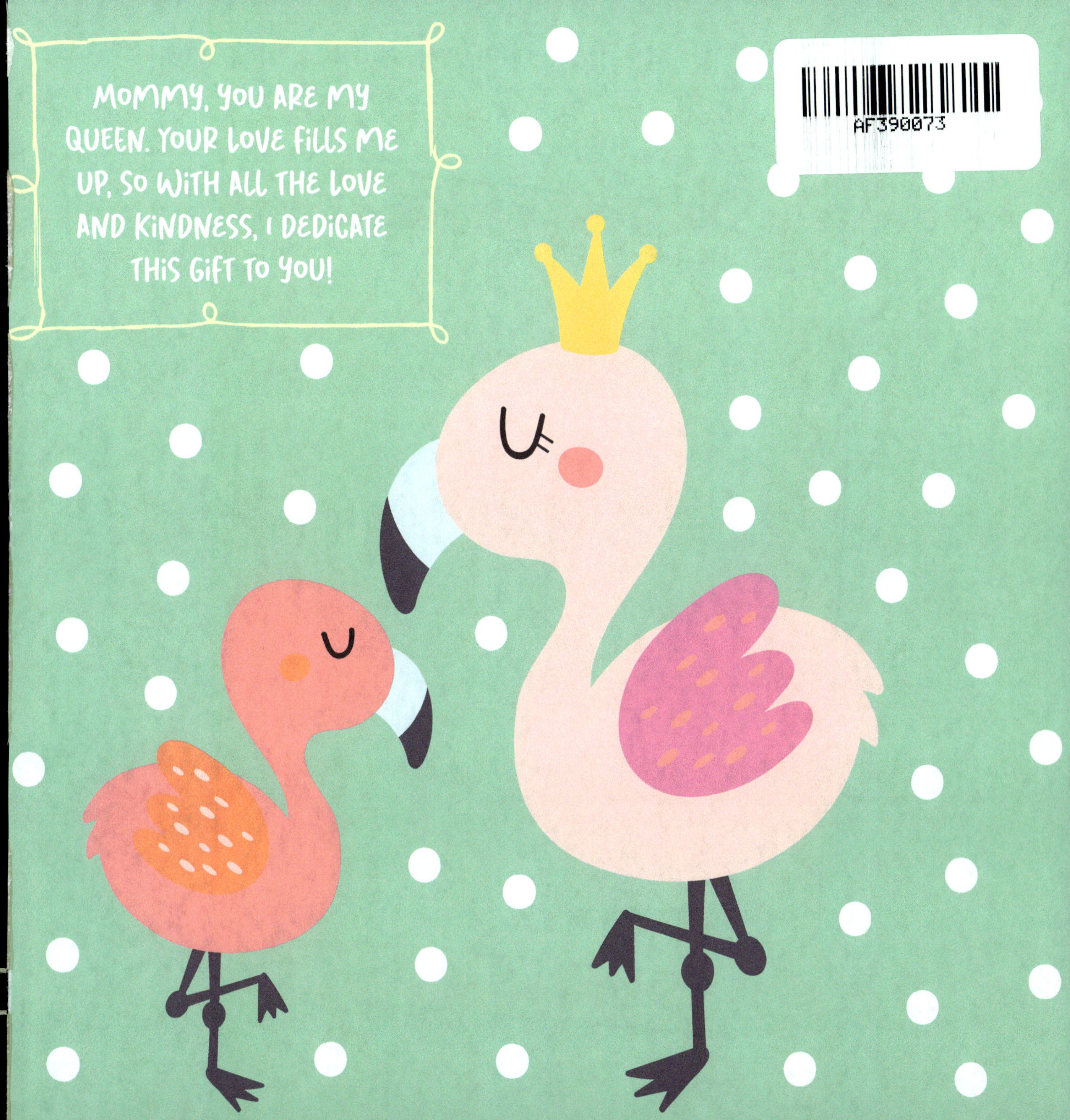
MOMMY, YOU ARE MY QUEEN. YOUR LOVE FILLS ME UP, SO WITH ALL THE LOVE AND KINDNESS, I DEDICATE THIS GIFT TO YOU!
AF390073

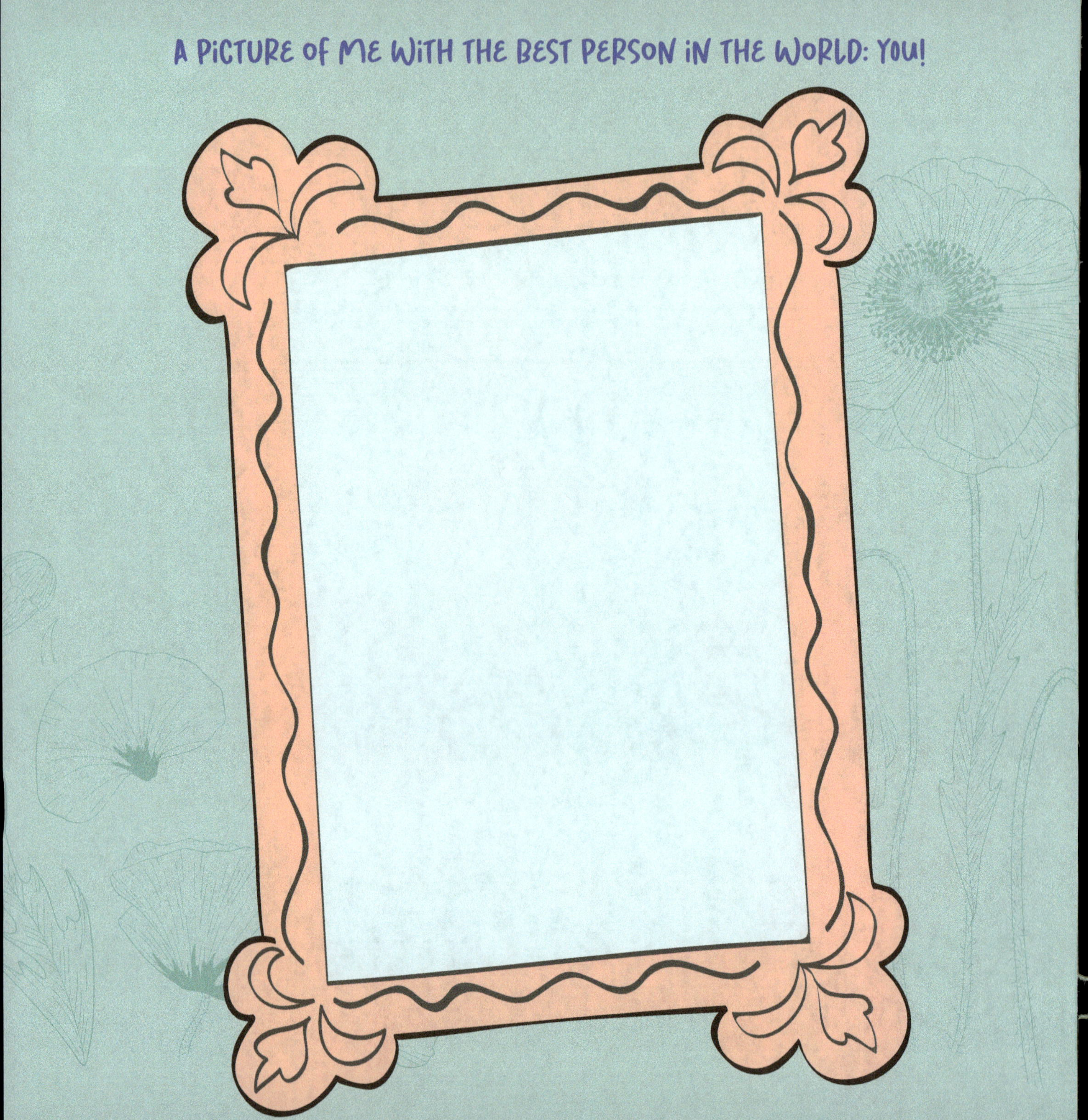

A PICTURE OF ME WITH THE BEST PERSON IN THE WORLD: YOU!

MOMMY, YOU HAVE TAKEN SO MANY PICTURES OF ME!
HERE I WANT TO KEEP THE MOST SPECIAL OF THEM ALL!

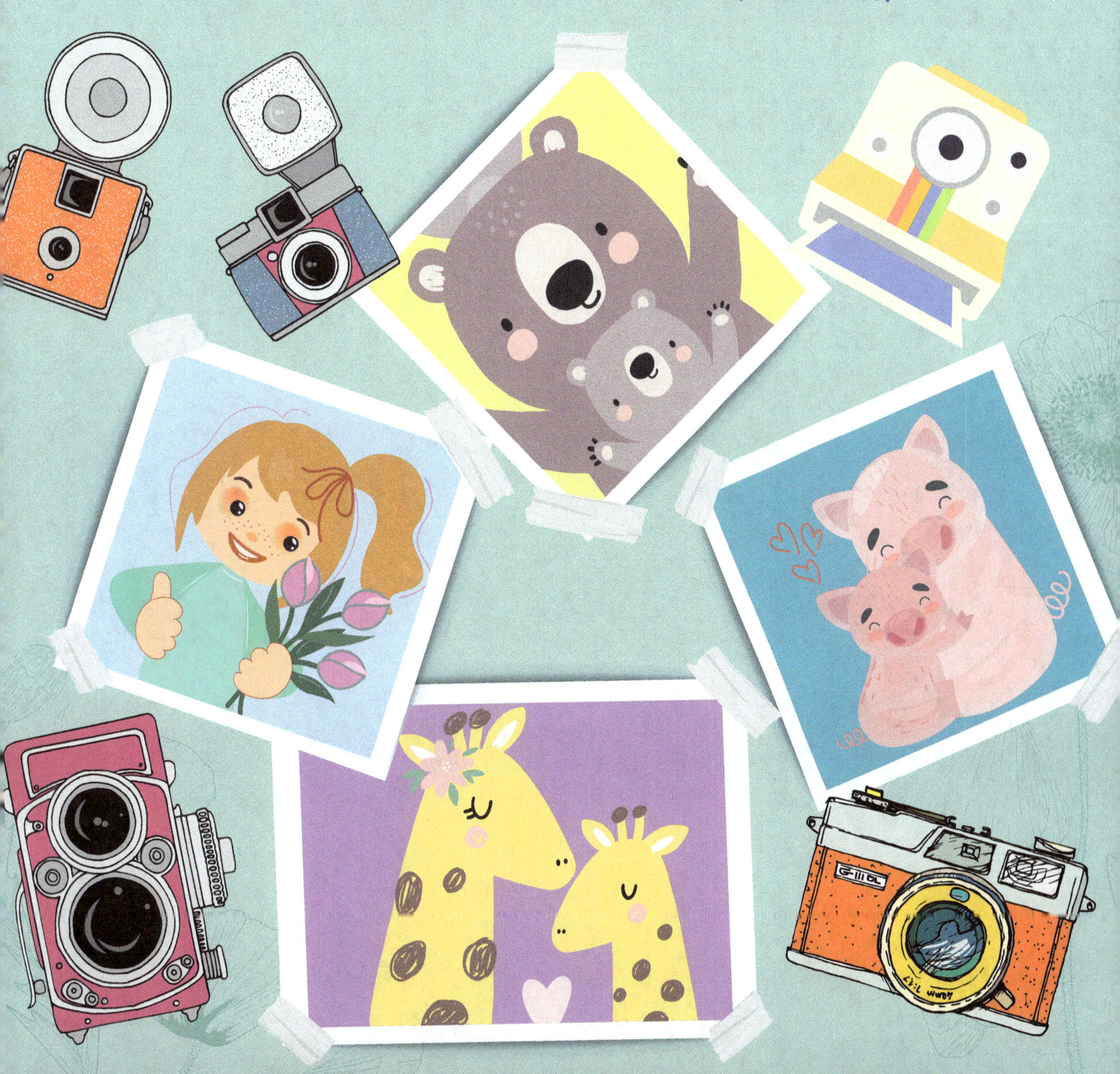

WHEN I WAS BORN...
DAY:
I WEIGHED:
MY HEIGHT WAS:

AND TODAY...
DAY:
MY WEIGH IS:
MY HEIGHT IS:

MOMMY WAS____YEARS OLD.   NOW SHE IS____YEARS OLD.

MOMMY, THIS PIECE OF STRING REPRESENTS MY HEIGHT.
I USED IT TO MAKE A BEAUTIFUL DRAWING FOR YOU!

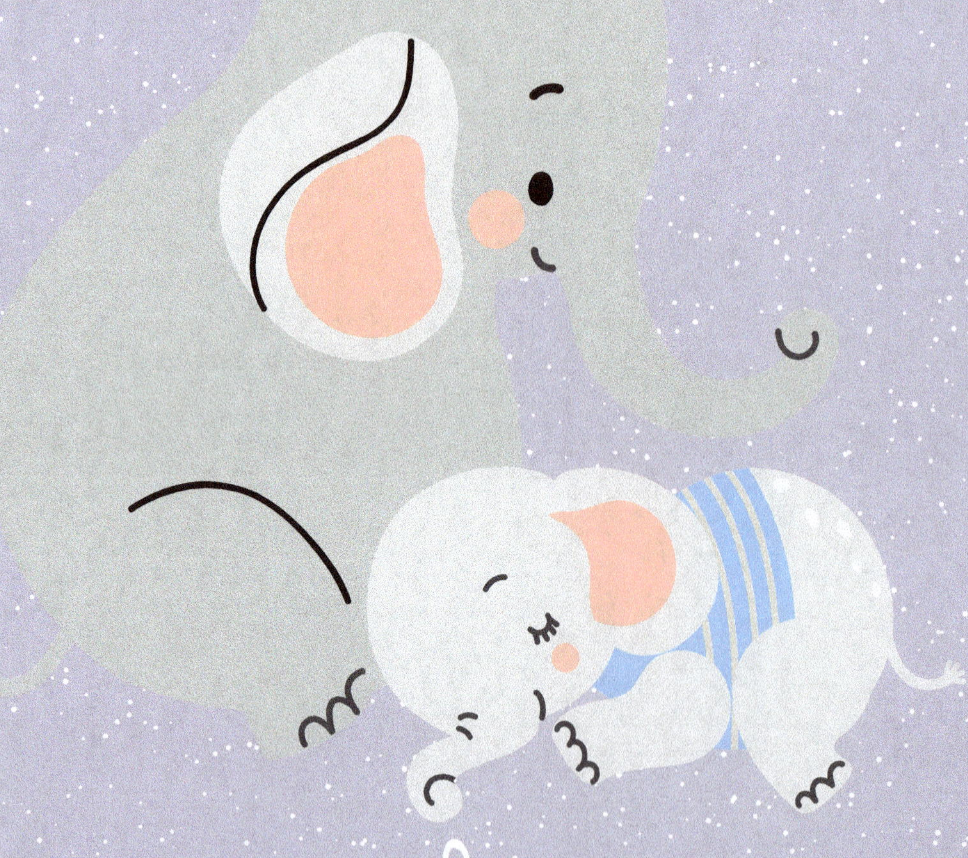
OH, MOMMY... SO MUCH HAS CHANGED
SINCE THE DAY I WAS BORN, RIGHT?
LET'S REMEMBER TOGETHER.

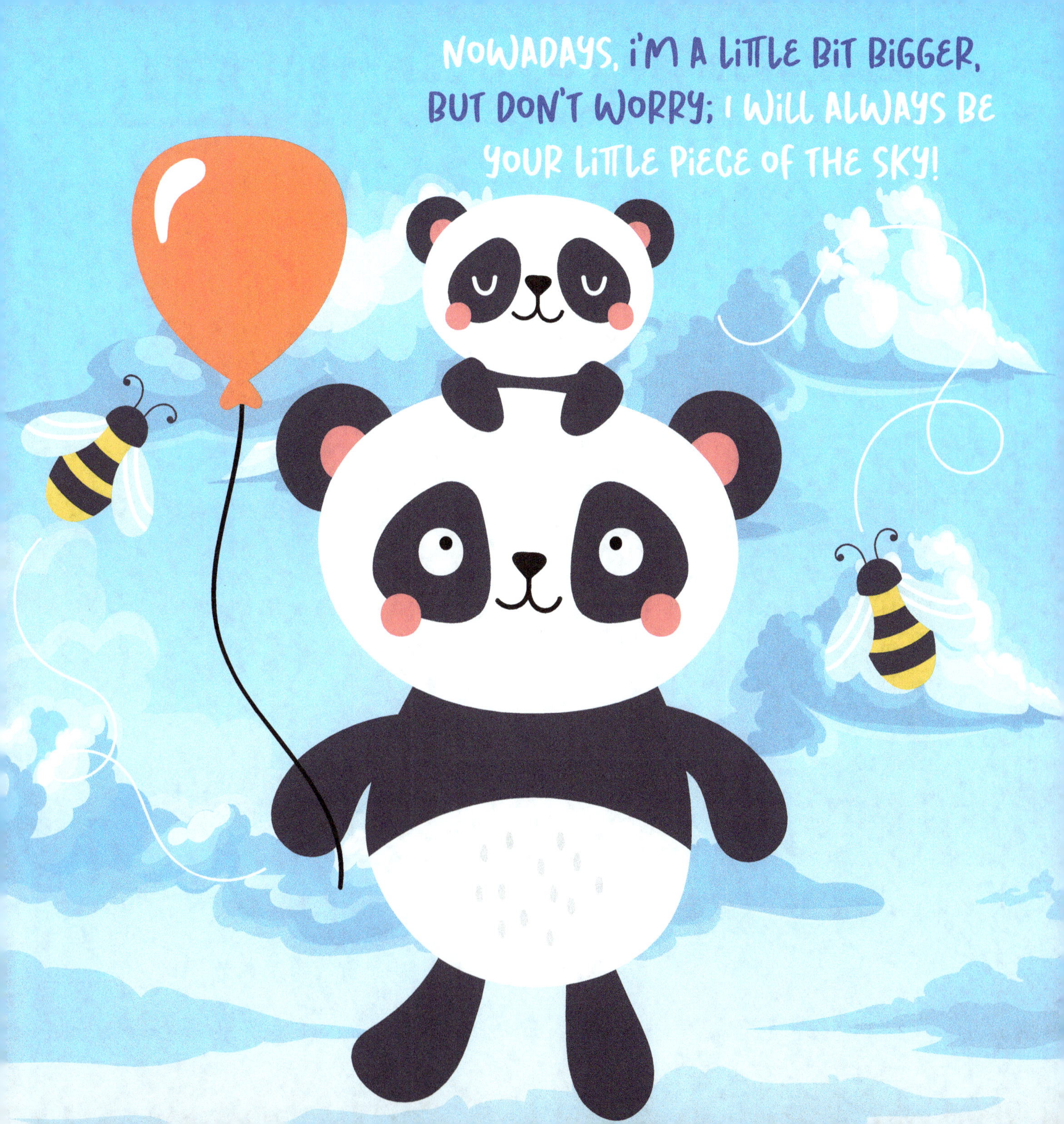
NOWADAYS, I'M A LITTLE BIT BIGGER,
BUT DON'T WORRY; I WILL ALWAYS BE
YOUR LITTLE PIECE OF THE SKY!

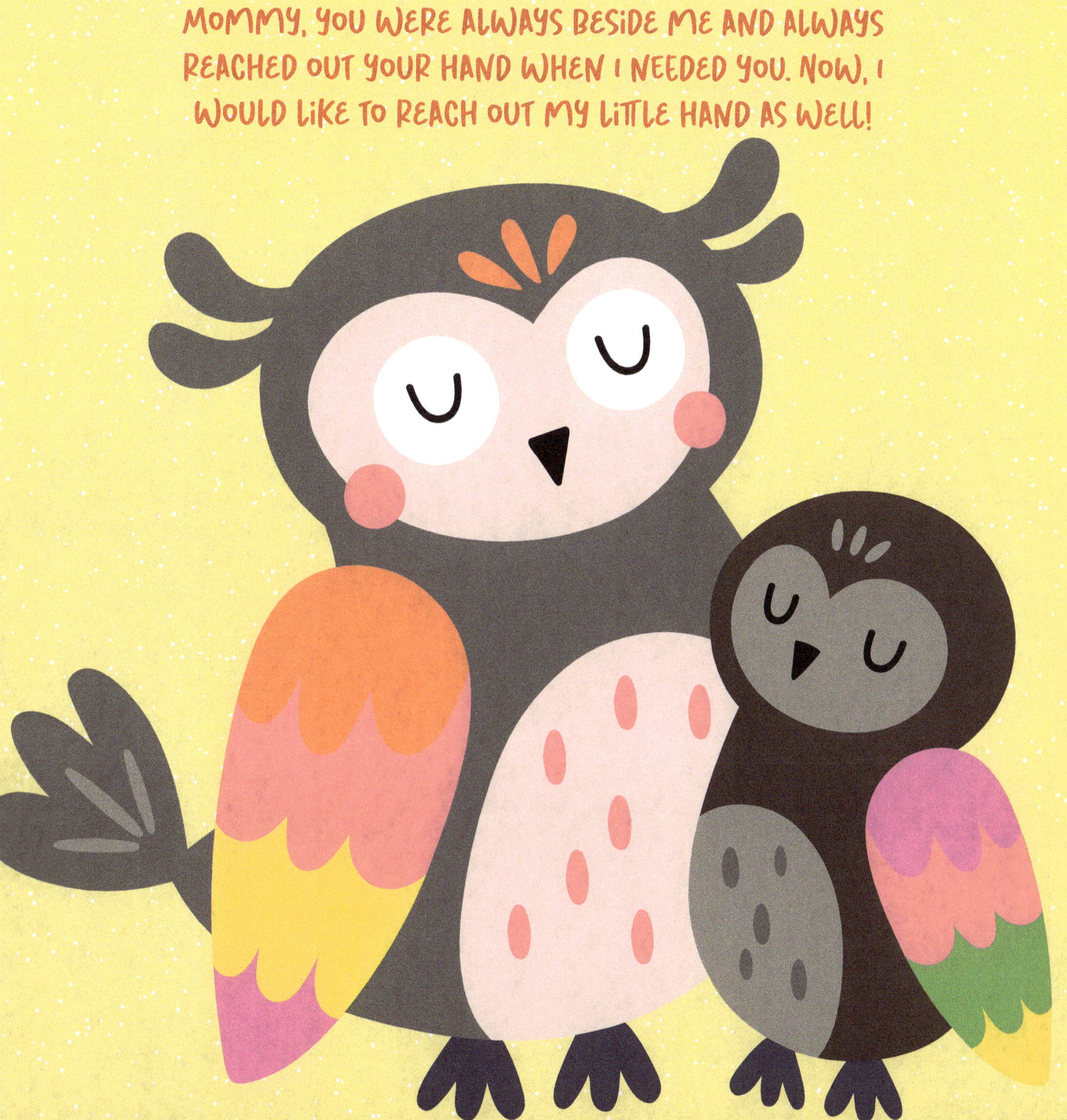
MOMMY, YOU WERE ALWAYS BESIDE ME AND ALWAYS REACHED OUT YOUR HAND WHEN I NEEDED YOU. NOW, I WOULD LIKE TO REACH OUT MY LITTLE HAND AS WELL!

HERE IS A DRAWING OF ONE OF THE MOST FUN GAMES THAT WE PLAYED TOGETHER:

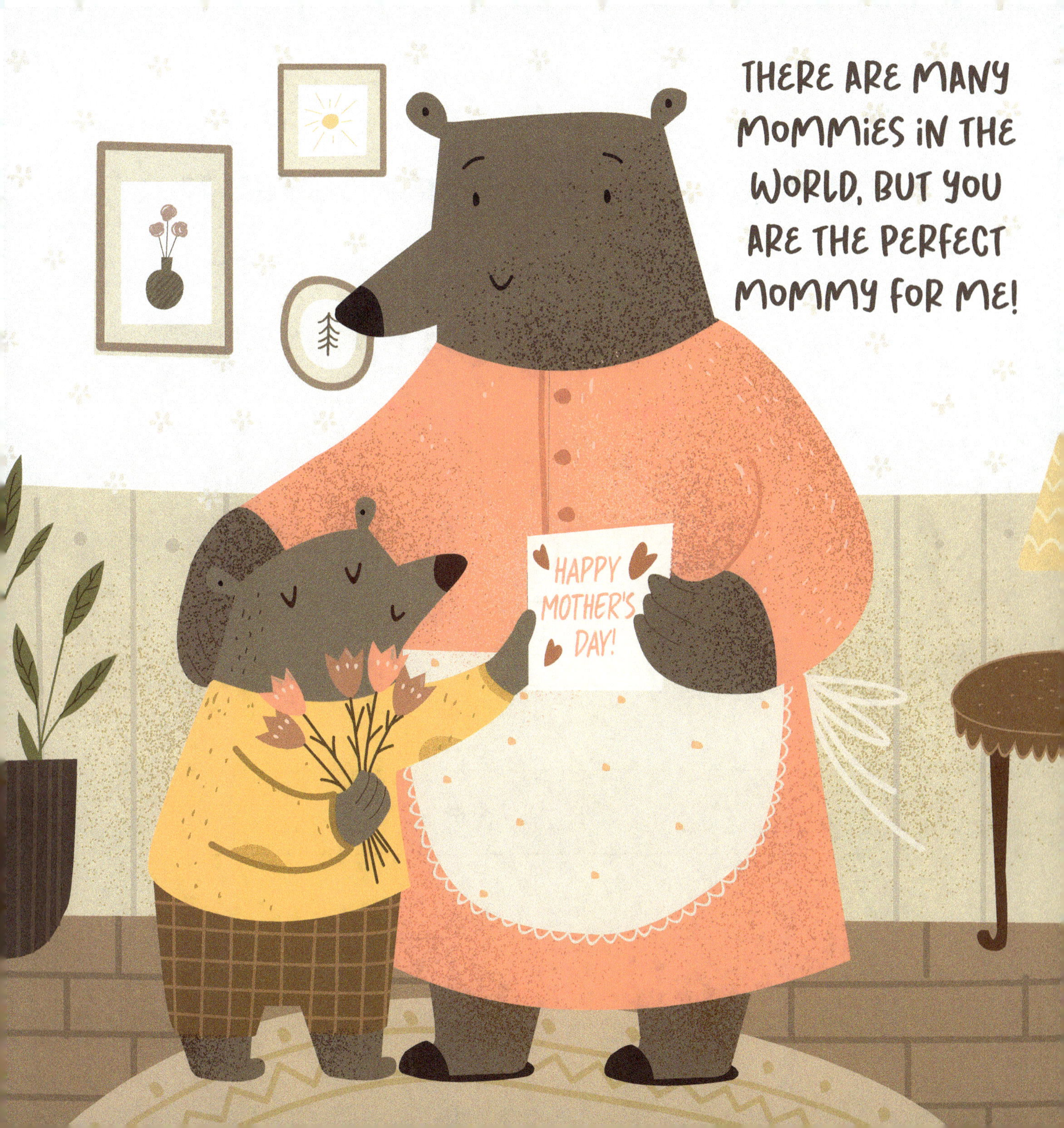

THERE ARE MANY MOMMIES IN THE WORLD, BUT YOU ARE THE PERFECT MOMMY FOR ME!
HAPPY MOTHER'S DAY!

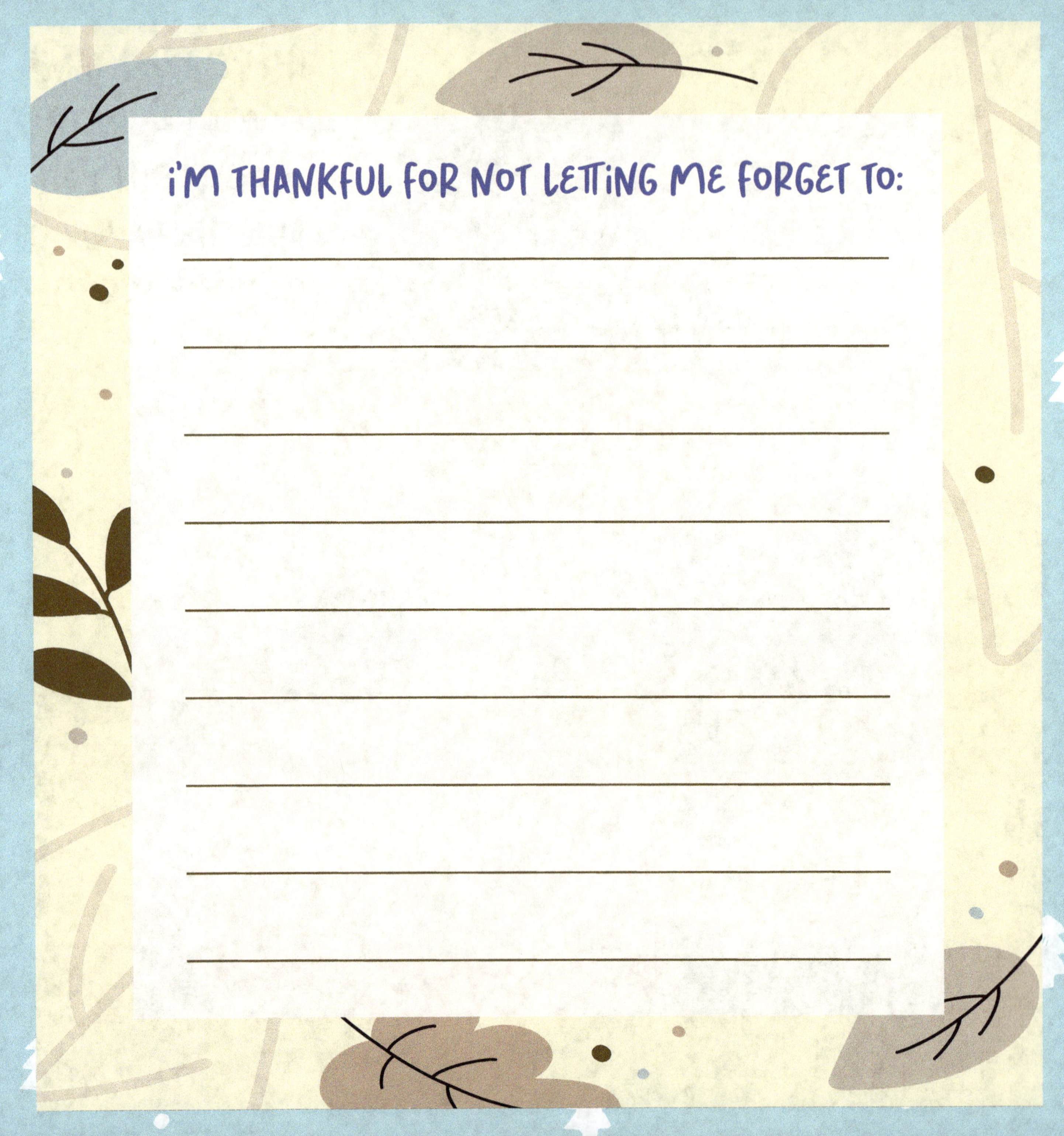
i'M THANKFUL FOR NOT LETTING ME FORGET TO:

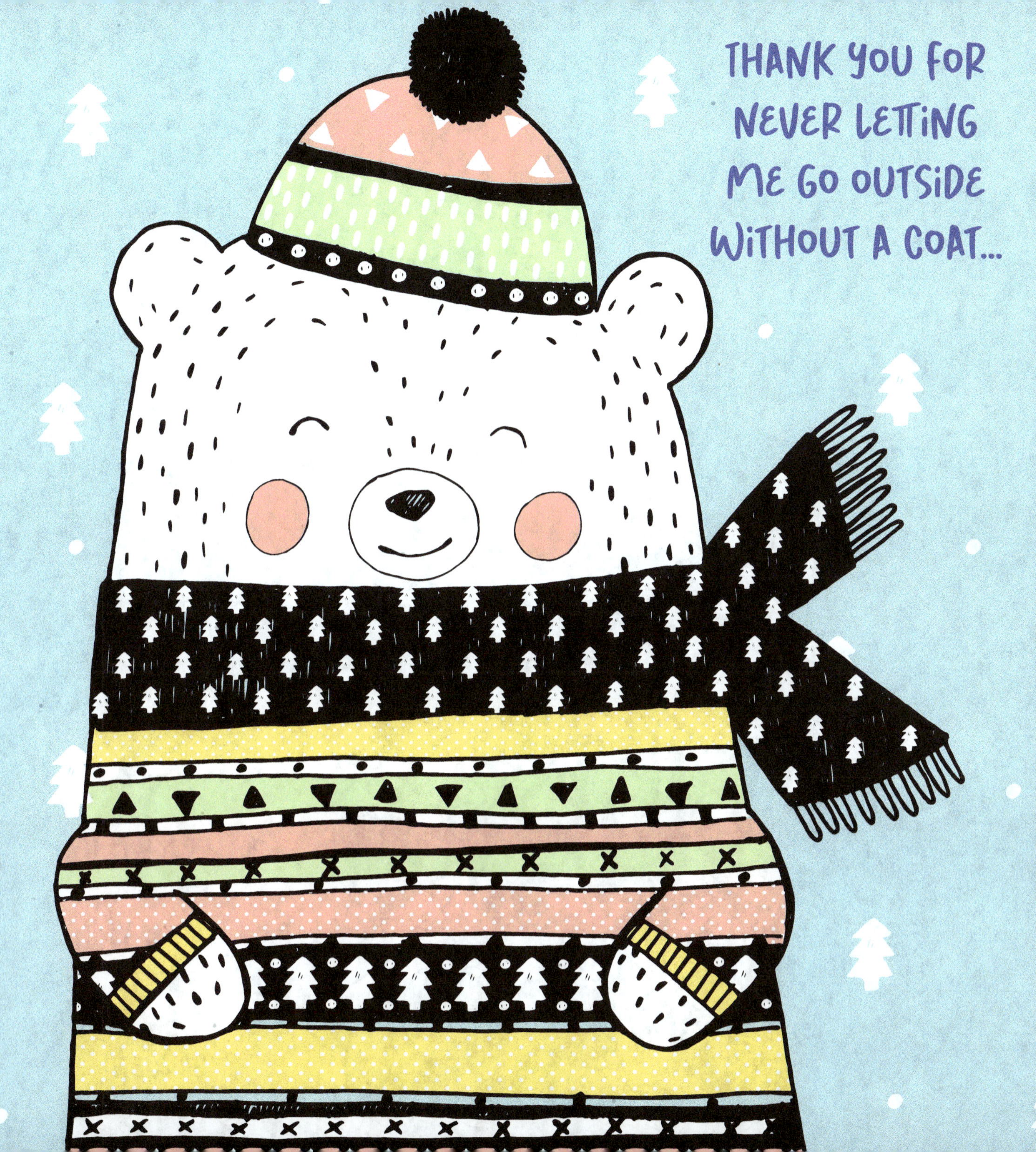

THANK YOU FOR
NEVER LETTING
ME GO OUTSIDE
WITHOUT A COAT...

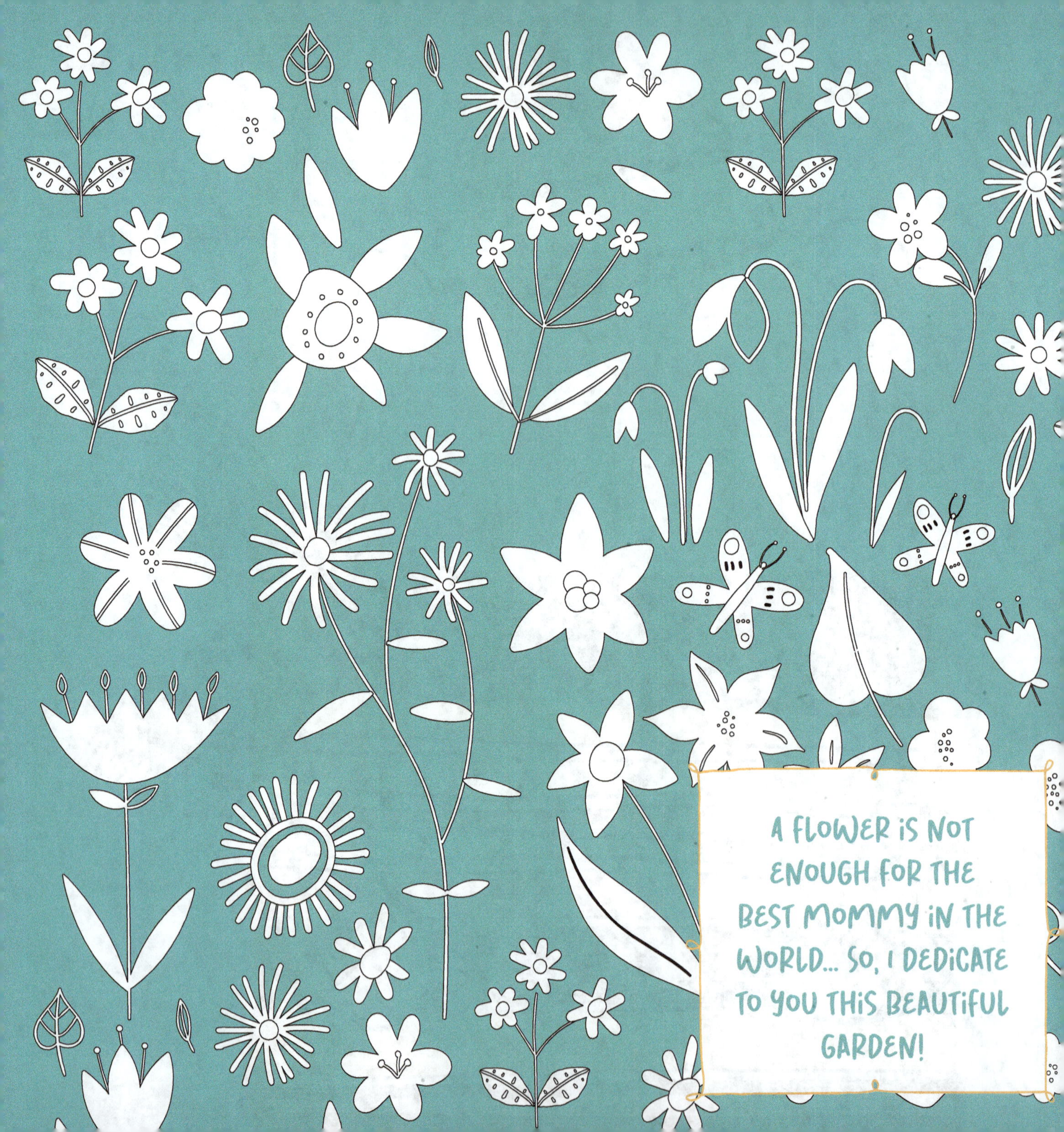
A FLOWER IS NOT ENOUGH FOR THE BEST MOMMY IN THE WORLD... SO, I DEDICATE TO YOU THIS BEAUTIFUL GARDEN!

YOU TAUGHT ME THAT I AM NOT EVERYONE. BUT, MOST IMPORTANTLY,
YOU TEACH ME EVERY DAY HOW TO BE THE BEST PERSON IN THE WORLD!

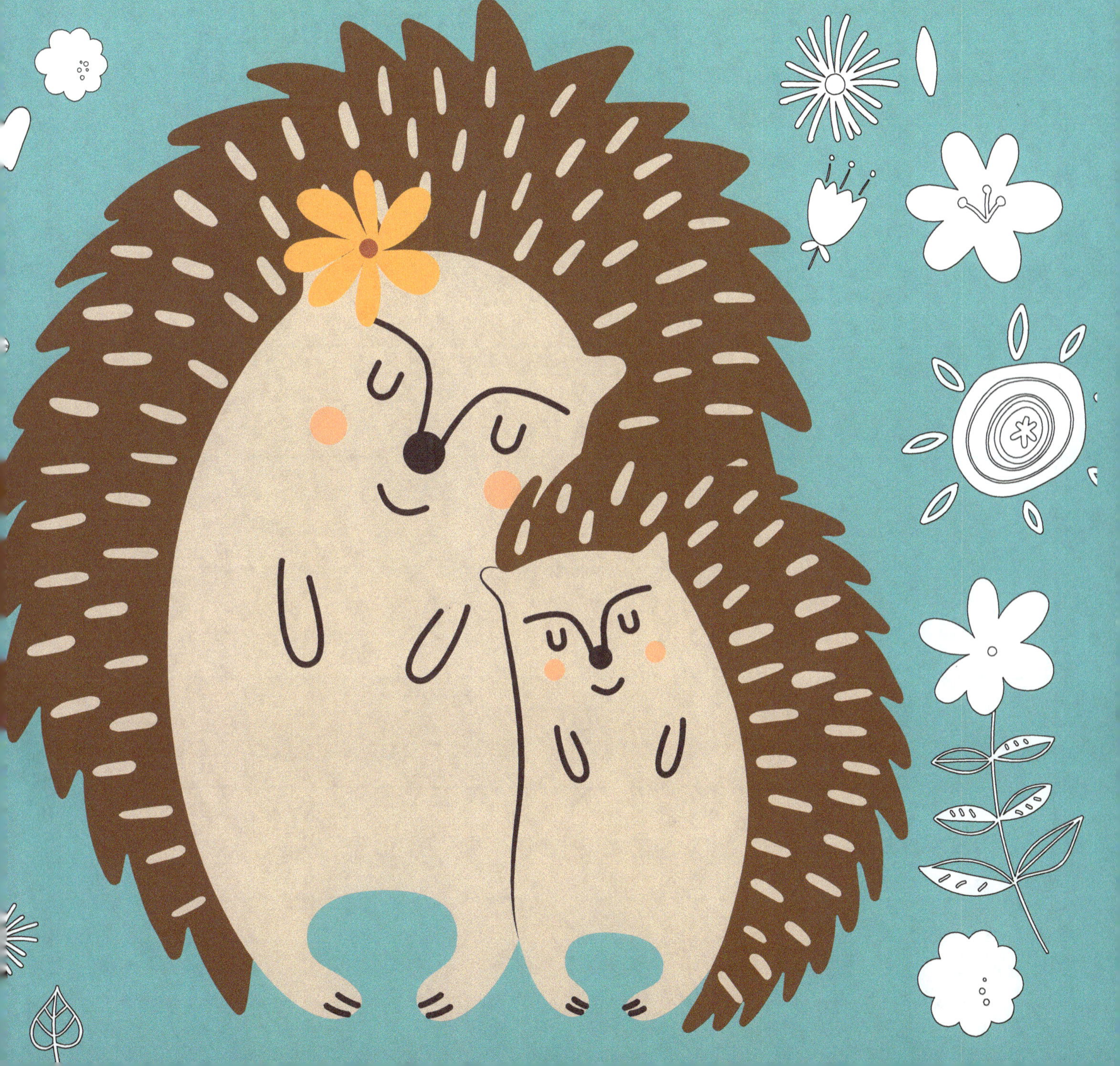

THANKS TO YOU, MOMMY, I ALSO LEARNED HOW TO:

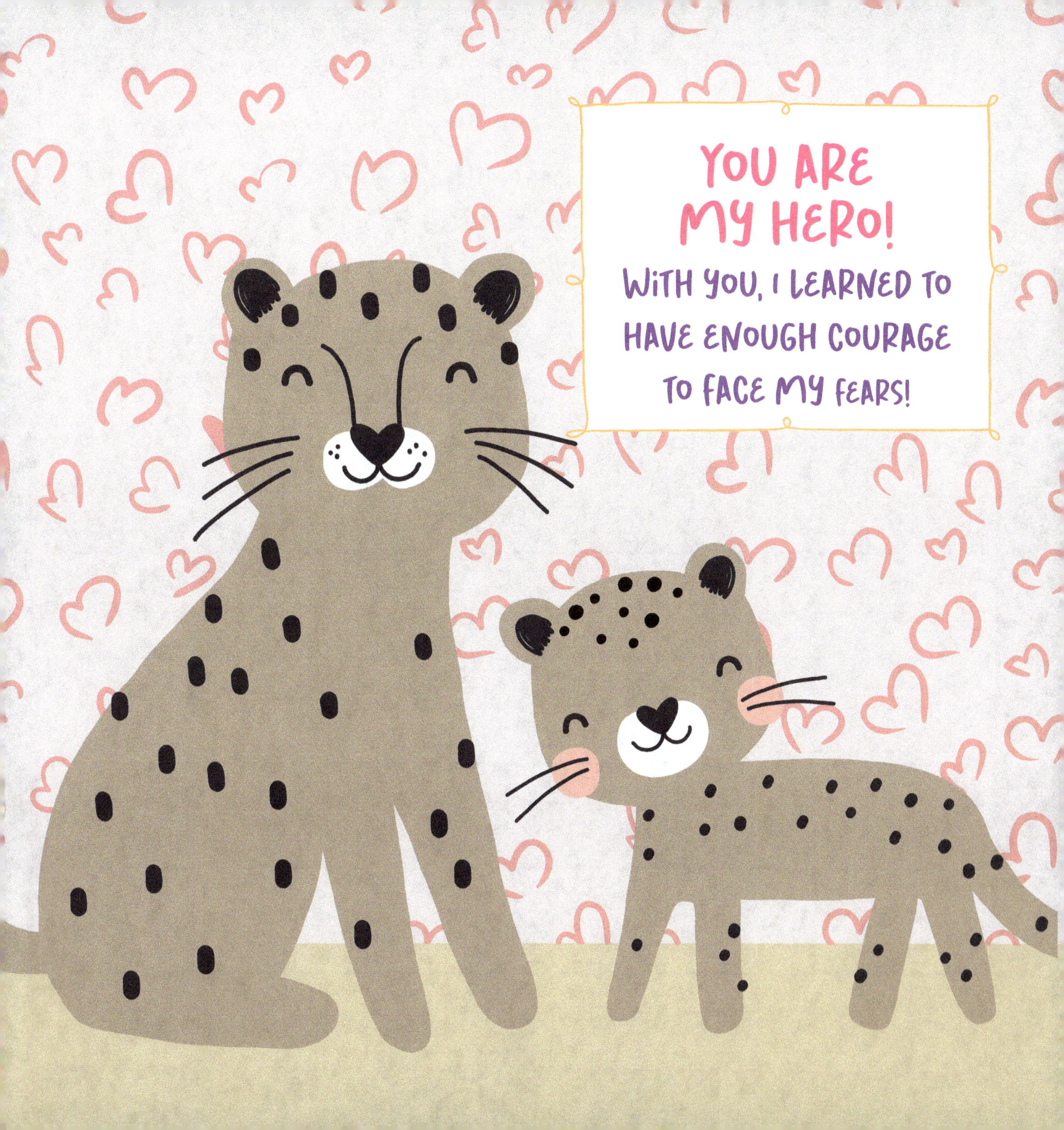

YOU ARE MY HERO!
WITH YOU, I LEARNED TO HAVE ENOUGH COURAGE TO FACE MY FEARS!

HERE I LEAVE A MESSAGE FULL OF LOVE
FOR YOU TO READ ON YOUR HARD DAYS.

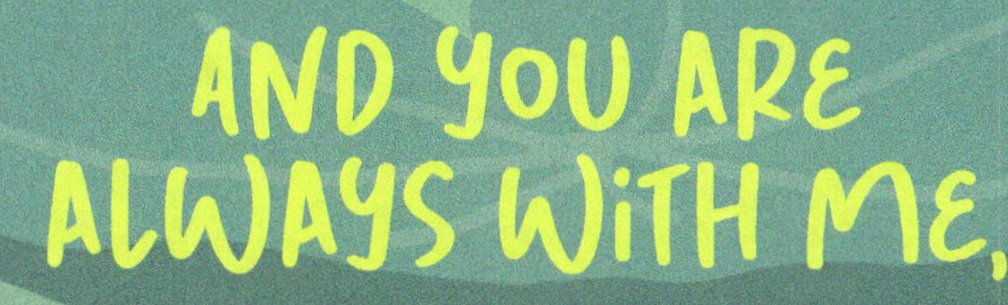
AND YOU ARE
ALWAYS WITH ME,

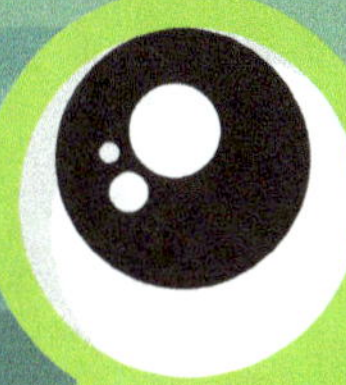

IN THE GOOD MOMENTS
AND IN THE HARD
MOMENTS TOO.

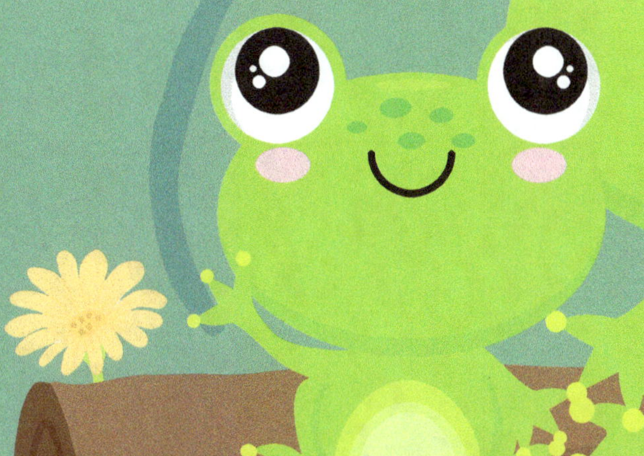

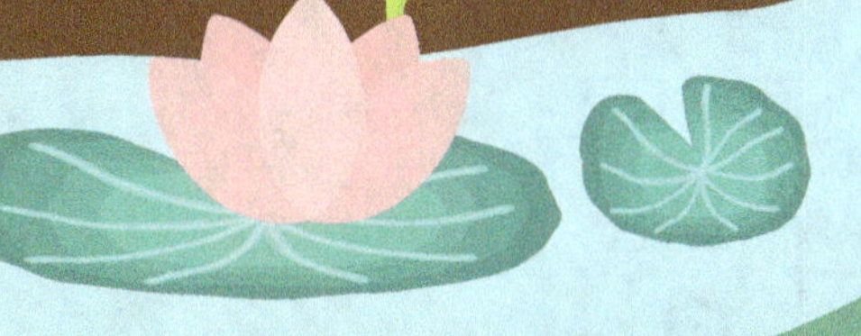

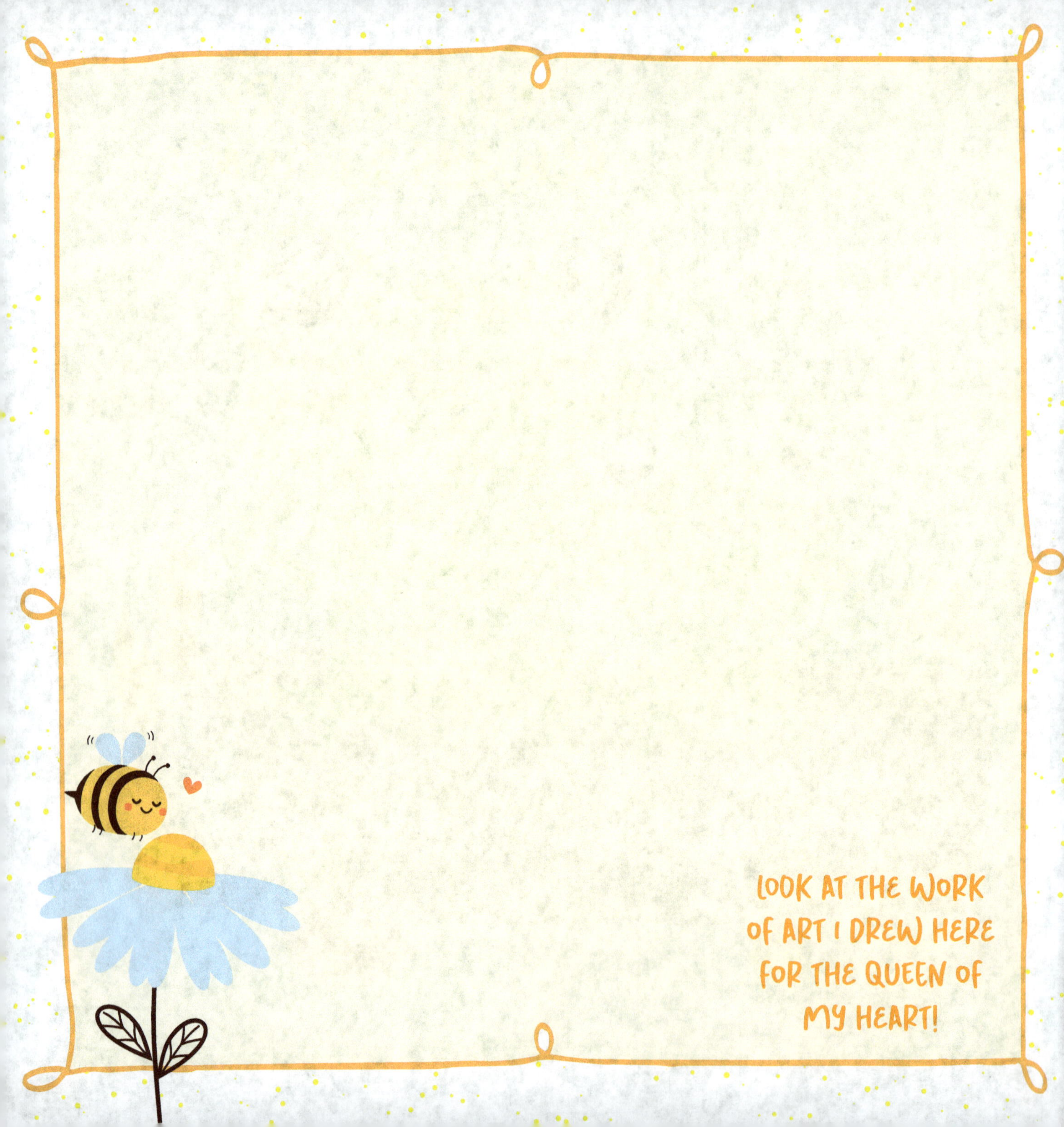
LOOK AT THE WORK
OF ART I DREW HERE
FOR THE QUEEN OF
MY HEART!

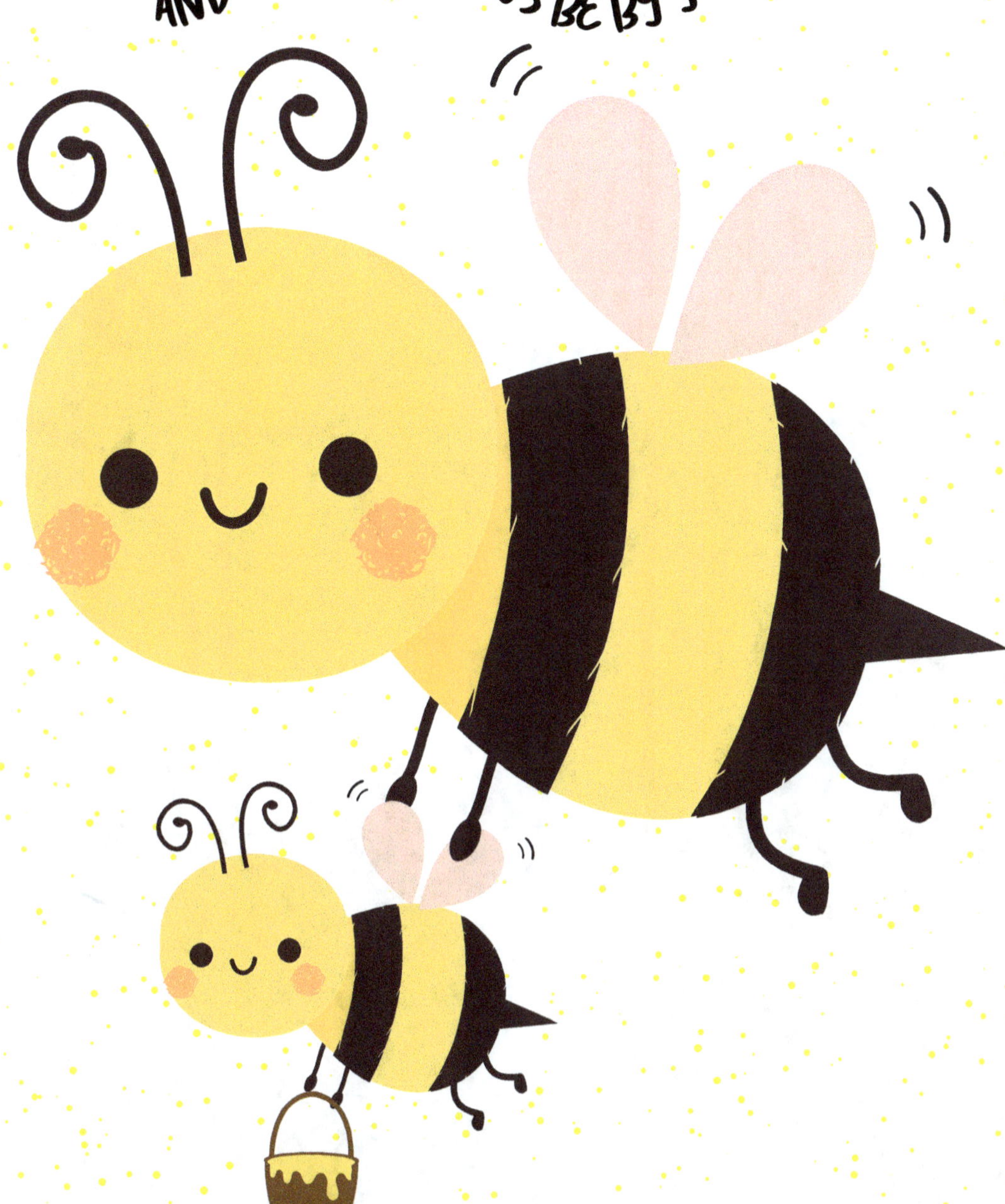

YOU ARE MY QUEEN BEE
AND I WILL ALWAYS BE BY YOUR SIDE!

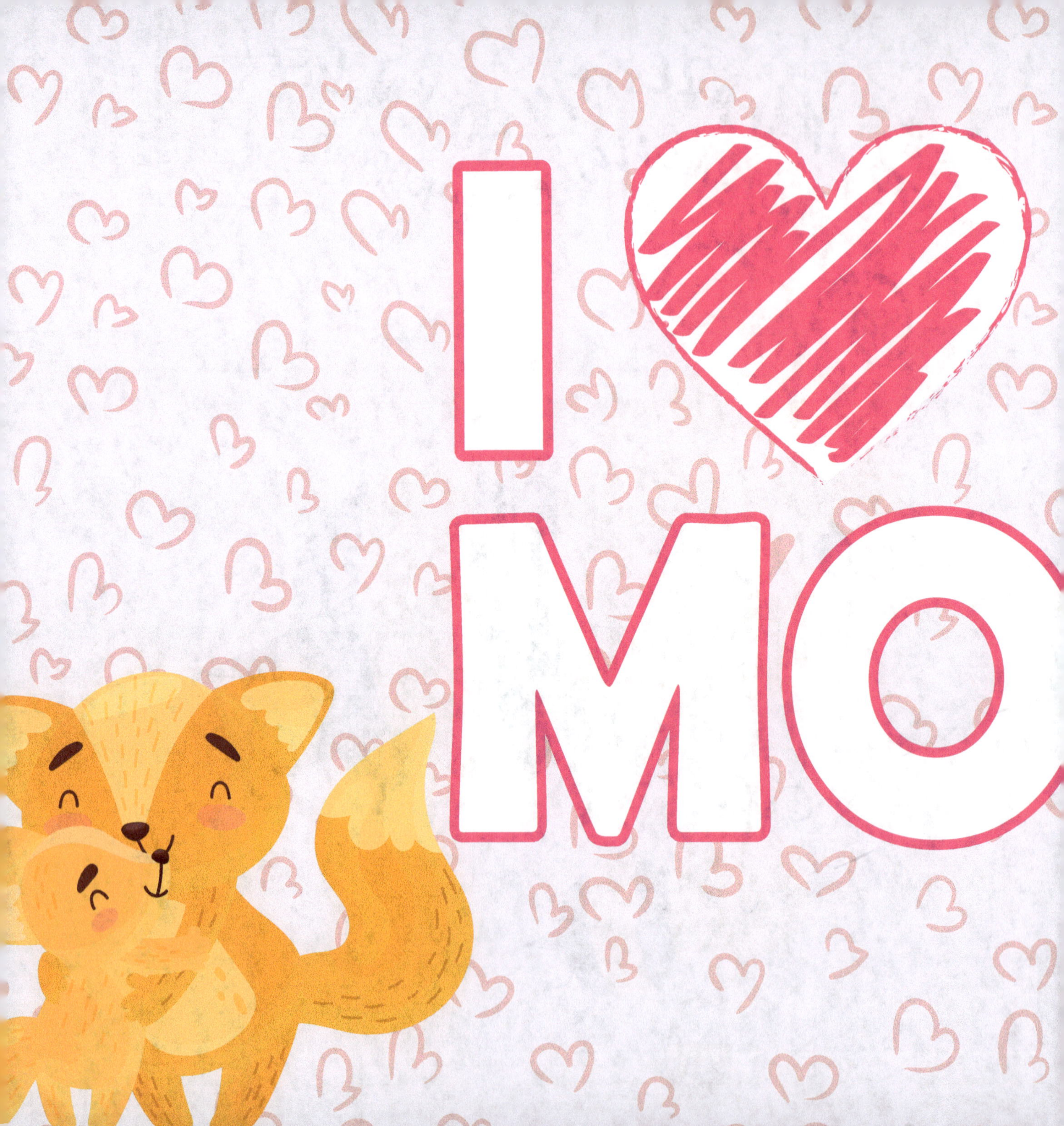

I ♥ MO

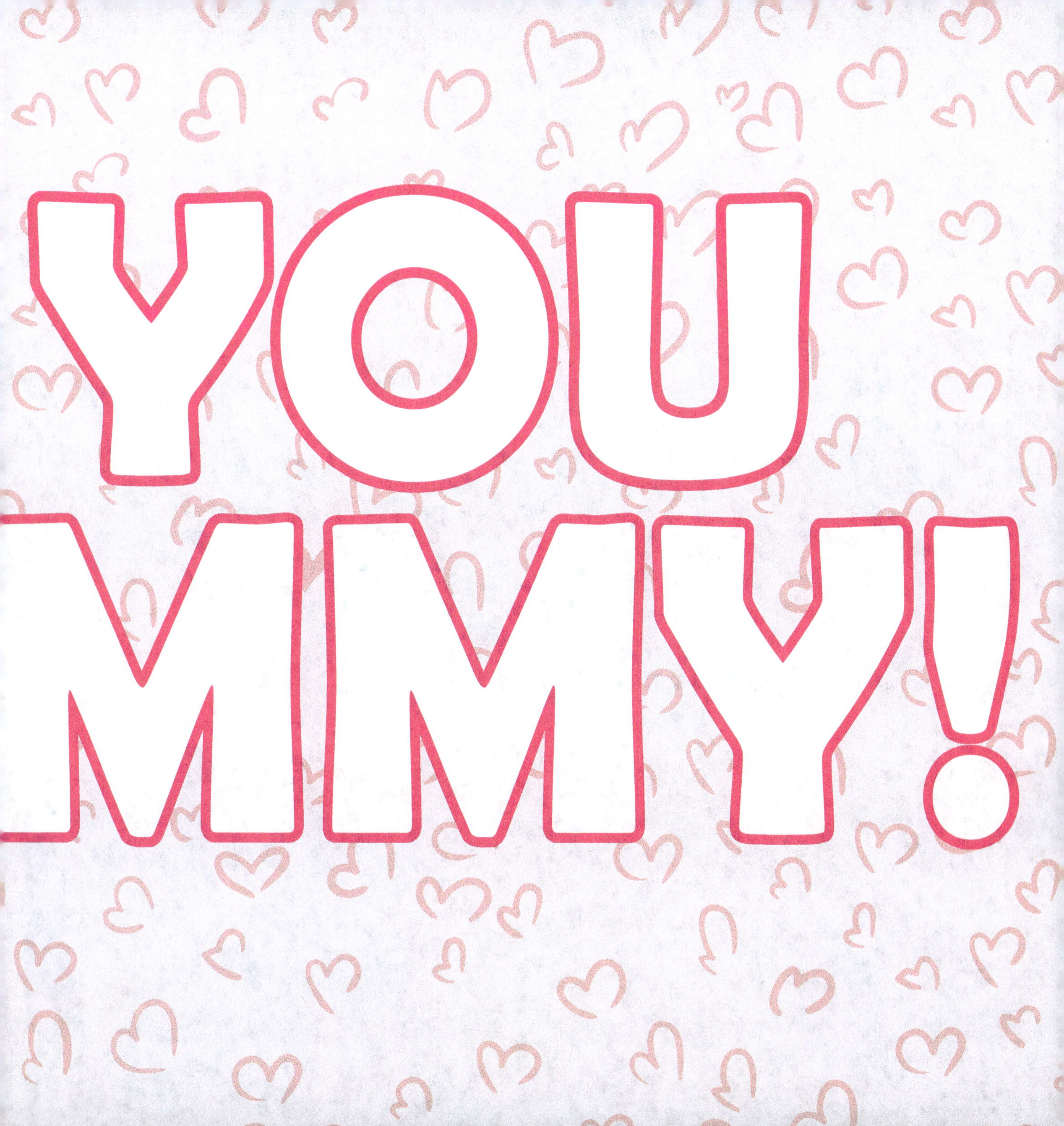

YOU
MMY!

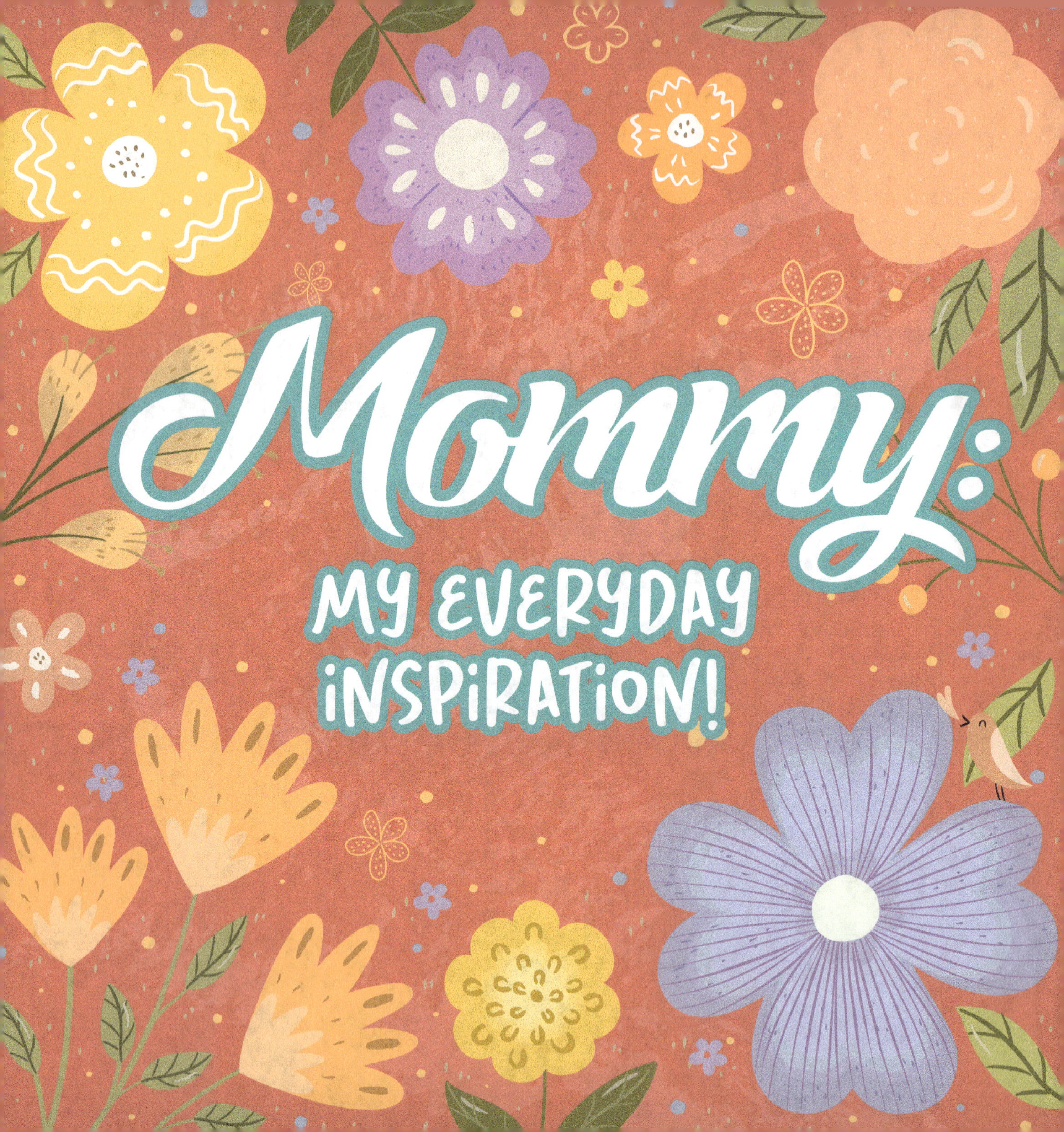

Mommy:
MY EVERYDAY
INSPIRATION!